MW00762849

LIVING *with*
GOOD MANNERS

This is a translation of *El libro joven de la gente con clase* copyright
© 2015 Ediciones Rialp, S.A., Madrid

English translation, copyright © 2016 Scepter Publishers, Inc.

The total or partial reproduction of this book is not permitted, nor its
informatic treatment, or the transmission of any form or by any means, either
electronic, mechanic, photocopy or other methods, without the prior written
permission of the owners of the copyright.

Published by Scepter Publishers, Inc.
info@scepterpublishers.org
www.scepterpublishers.org
800-322-8773
New York

All rights reserved.

Translated by Tamara Urcia
Text and cover design by Carol S. Cates

Printed in the United States of America
ISBN: 978-1-59417-260-1

Library of Congress Cataloging-in-Publication Data

Names: Narbona, John, author.
Title: Living with good manners : a handbook for young people with class /
    John Narbona.
Other titles: Libro joven de la gente con clase. English
Description: 1 [edition]. | New York : Scepter Publishers, 2016.
Identifiers: LCCN 2016033644 | ISBN 9781594172601 (pbk. : alk. paper)
Subjects: LCSH: Etiquette for young adults.
Classification: LCC BJ1857.Y58 N3713 2016 | DDC 395.1/24--dc23
LC record available at https://lccn.loc.gov/2016033644

Library of Congress LCCN Permalink for 2016033644
lccn.loc.gov
LCCN Permalink provides persistent links to metadata records in the
LC Online Catalog. LCCN: 2016033644

LIVING *with* GOOD MANNERS

A HANDBOOK *for*

YOUNG PEOPLE WITH CLASS

John Narbona

Scepter

Take care of your interior as well as your exterior,
because both make up the one person that is you.
BUDDHA

Only those with good manners are truly free.
EPICTETO

CONTENTS

1

OBJECTIONS TO GOOD MANNERS

1. "They're just a bunch of social conventions." It's true; many of them could be different. But they're universally valued and accepted. If you follow them, you'll see that they make sense.

2. "They're worthless." That's not true—manners show your worth. Others will form a good opinion of you, and manners will give you more confidence in your daily life.

3. "I should be free to be myself!" Of course! But being yourself could mean acting like a Neanderthal or a courageous, elegant person. You decide.

4. "Just let me have fun while I'm young." To have a good time and to be well-mannered aren't incompatible. To be young is to be creative, original, and eager, but it's not a free ticket to act like an animal (although many may try to convince you otherwise).

5. "OK, but there are way too many rules." That's true. In fact, it's almost impossible to follow them all, and it doesn't matter if you make a mistake. Don't worry, you'll learn little by little. It's like a soccer player who is amazing with the ball. No one knows how he does it. He's simply that good because he's practiced so much.

6. "What if I'm the only one who behaves this way?" What do you prefer to be? A lion or just another sheep among the fold? Strive for the first option, even if others don't follow your example.

2

INTRODUCTION: TO FLY LIKE THE EAGLES

An author once suggested, "Don't fly like a cooped up bird when you can fly like an eagle."

In other words, do you want to be like a chicken or like an eagle? Like an eagle, of course! You want to fly high, but in order to do that, you have to be different from the crowd. Thousands of young people work hard, study languages, are lots of fun, understand music, and so on, but they don't know how to behave in public. Sometimes it's the small details that set you apart.

People have been practicing good manners for centuries. In medieval times, someone who was well-mannered could become a "knight" or a "lady"—someone who was appreciated for courage, nobility, and good upbringing. (Yes, yes, the "ladies," too! Besides sewing and playing instruments, they were courageous. Remember Marian, Robin Hood's betrothed.)

Just as these knights defended just causes with a lance, a sword, and a shield, good manners can help you fight against other dragons: your unpleasant character, your shyness, or your fear of making a fool of yourself, obstacles that often prevent you from dreaming big dreams.

Persons who act with confidence (because they know how to eat properly, match their clothes well, speak in public without trembling, or make amends after making a mistake) are capable of surpassing their own expectations. Good manners will keep you from getting carried away by your emotions, help you see the good in others, and live more comfortably and elegantly.

Over and over again I hear people say, "This book is a waste of time. Young people will do as they please; they don't like to follow the rules." Those who talk like that have little trust in you. They see you as the children you once were rather than as the men and women you wish to become. It's true that you still don't know yourself very well and you'll still make plenty of mistakes, but it's enough that you have a strong desire to be a better person.

Of course, if you read this whole book all at once, it might remind you of your mother nagging at you, saying, "Don't do that! Don't sit like that! Don't bite your fingernails! Don't be late!" Well, your mother is right, but because you know she loves you so much, you might take her for granted and not listen to a thing she says. But don't worry. Even though good manners may seem like a pain in the beginning, in the end they will make you freer.

You may notice that many norms have to do with self-control (controlling your emotions and impulses, how you use technology, deal with your physical needs, and so on) It's all about learning to control yourself and not to be controlled.

Have you ever flown a kite with two strings? If you have, you may remember the incredible feeling of controlling an object more than fifty yards above you that is sustained only by the wind. A slight movement of your hand was enough to make it pirouette to the right or to the left. Similarly, if you're able to control yourself through good manners and form your body and your will to want what is good, your life will be a beautiful pirouette.

So learn these rules, but calmly. At times, you might be able to skip one or two without any problem at all. And don't become a drill sergeant by demanding others to follow norms of good behavior they've never heard of, either! The good example you give to others and a little bit of patience is enough. Just use common sense.

If you begin living out the most important ones, the

rest will follow naturally. Very quickly you'll be very proud of your life and you'll see yourself in a whole new light. Elegance, especially internal elegance, is captivating. Without knowing it, you'll begin speaking a sort of "secret language" with your personality that will attract—and allow you to choose—those truly worth your time.

3

LADIES AND GENTLEMEN

I must admit that I have certain heroes when it comes to elegance. My male hero is James Bond, the secret agent of Her Majesty, the Queen of England. He never loses his composure amid bombshells and gunfire throughout an entire two-hour movie. If we are talking about ladies, there's no other actress like Audrey Hepburn. She's always calm, joyful, and elegant. OK, I know her movies are older than dirt, but look up a few scenes on YouTube and you'll see that this kind of class doesn't go out of style. It's timeless.

I mention both of these movie characters in order to show you that certain norms of behavior, although few, pertain to men and others to women. Good manners, among other things, make men more manly and women more womanly. The two sexes share the great majority of rules, but a few are specific to men or to women. So that each one pays more attention to his or her particular area, certain suggestions pertaining especially to guys will be designated by a drawing of a gentleman with a top hat, mustache, and glasses next to it (yes, it's James Bond in disguise). If the suggestion is especially for the gals, you'll see a picture of a lady with a formal hat and glasses next to it (the elegant Audrey Hepburn, of course).

Even though good behavior usually comes from within, it must be practiced in many different circumstances. For that reason, I have divided this book into chapters that correspond to particular places or contexts: for example, dealing with other people, personal hygiene, guys and gals, the beach, the movies, and so on.

There are three levels of etiquette—basic, intermediate, and superior.

Basic: These rules are impossible not to know. Even whales follow them, although they have no idea what they are.

Intermediate: These suggestions make a good impression. Following them will place you an inch above the rest, which is generally enough.

Superior: James Bond and Audrey Hepburn are in this category, which is for those who want to conquer the world!

★ ★ ★

I hope this book will help you discover the great spirit inside of you and show you how it can grow by your interactions with others.

4

NOT ONLY FOR YOUNG PEOPLE

For those who live with young people on a daily basis (parents, family members, teachers), this manual attempts to transmit some clear and practical advice for helping young men and women live the basic norms of etiquette every day.

Most adults have lived long enough to realize how many doors and hearts are opened by good manners. They also know through personal experience that good etiquette is directly related to happiness. Because living good manners allows young people to be more confident, better persons in their daily lives, practicing good manners will make them proud of themselves. You'll be able to perceive that they're capable of controlling themselves and doing great things.

You can help them through your good example and remind them not to get discouraged or lose their patience. It's not a simple task to learn good manners all at once. The following phrase is attributed to Confucius: "They told me and I forgot; I saw it and understood it; I did it and mastered it." The young people who read these pages will learn good manners by practicing them, but they'll practice them only if they see them lived out in those around them. In sum, being a good example is the only way what is written in this book will not be forgotten.

5

DEALING WITH OTHERS

In everyday life

"Thank you" are two words that make all the difference. To thank others for small acts of service throughout the day is a sign of greatness. So thank the teenager at McDonald's who brings out your food, the neighbor who waits for you to get on the elevator, your mom who makes you a snack, the friend who subs for you as goalie during the soccer game, the friend who lends you her notes, the cashier at the store, etc. "I'm sorry" and "please" are other magic words that are often more effective than Harry Potter's most powerful spells.

Good manners apply to how you use your body. It's healthy to stretch when you wake up in the morning, for example, but avoid doing it in front of others, especially at the table. Some people look just like Spider-man shooting webs across the Manhattan skyscrapers.

Sneezing and yawning are two uncontrollable bodily reactions. Nevertheless, it's best to minimize the damages. If you need to sneeze, do it moderately and without shouting a war cry. Humanity has suffered through enough atomic bombs! If you have a tissue (note: carry a package of tissues), use it when you sneeze. Yawning is the right of every student, but you should yawn with elegance. Put your hand over your mouth so you don't expose your pearly whites to the entire universe.

If a sneeze comes on suddenly and without warning, cover your mouth and sneeze without shouting like Tarzan. If you sneeze on your hands, wipe them off with a tissue (did I mention you should carry tissues?), and wash your hands as soon as possible. Don't wipe them off on your pants or your coat. Whoever you're with will thank you for it. Never, ever look at your tissue after blowing your nose. What are you expecting to find? Gasoline? Sniffing is also very disagreeable to others. Besides, owing to the Earth's gravitational pull, you tend to have to repeat the action every forty or forty-five seconds. If you don't have a tissue, ask for one or look for a bathroom so you can take care of it.

Any outer demonstrations of inner functions like passing gas, burping, and spitting should be completely avoided when out in public. Even though some may think it's funny, on a deeper level it devalues the person who does them. The only difference between these folks and animals in the zoo is the cage. Out of self-respect, don't do any of these things in front of others. If the above-mentioned noises happen by accident, it's best to pretend they never happened or simply say, "Excuse me," and move on.

In a formal atmosphere, if you're suddenly overcome with an overwhelming itch, you must control yourself heroically. If you're unable to, you can excuse yourself for a moment. Once you're alone, you can scratch with the same calm as Cheetah, Tarzan's monkey. If you get the hiccups, it's not worth trying to hold them in. It's better to excuse yourself for a moment and try to stop them using the method that works best for you. (We all have our own remedies: hold your breath, drink something upside down without taking a breath, pinch your nose and swallow saliva, or startle yourself by looking at pictures of your parents when they were young.)

Biting your nails or cracking your knuckles (or your back) is not very elegant. Besides, if you do either of these repeatedly, it will create health problems and joint pain in the long run. Try to break the habit, both for your own good and because the sound of cracking bones isn't very pleasant to others.

If older women or elderly men drop something, go out of your way to pick it up for them (and return it to them, obviously). Do it for the ladies as an elegant gesture and for the men because it's painful for them to bend down.

Unless you're a member of a SWAT Team, which I seriously doubt, you should always knock on a closed or partially closed door before entering (and don't kick it down like the police do). The same rule applies in your own house. Of course, you should also wait a few seconds for someone to answer your knock before you open it.

Opening and closing doors is easy enough, but doing it with class requires a certain knack. Turning the knob all the way, push the door open; without letting go of the knob, close the door (without making the building fall down), and when it's completely closed, let go. Four simple steps: turn the knob, push the door, close the door, and let go. It seems easy, but you'll begin to notice that few people actually do it!

In an elevator, bus, or subway, let those inside get off before you get on, even though others may cut in front of you. It's always better to walk somewhere with dignity than fight like crazy zombies over the last seat on the bus.

If you're at someone else's house, keep these fundamental rules in mind: Don't wander around looking into all the rooms; don't open the refrigerator looking for something to scarf down; leave the bathroom clean, and take as little time as possible. You should also be attentive to when it's time for you to leave. Sometimes your friends' parents might start making indirect comments, such as observing how many things they have to do the next day, asking if it's getting a bit late, or sweeping under your chair with a broom. These may be signals that it's time to take off.

Complaining about having to go back to school or work after being on vacation is pretty lame. Some people complain so much you'd think they were on their way to the concentration camp at Auschwitz! Those who are sad make others sad along with them, which is bad form. Conversely, if you did well on an exam, admit it and move on. Those who burst into dramatic tears when they get a good grade soon become the brunt of others' jokes.

If you happen to notice someone in a potentially embarrassing situation (his zipper is down, there's a hole in the backside of his jeans, she has bird droppings in her hair), point it out to the person in private or with discreet gestures.

It's important to practice good manners with strangers but even more so with those we know. If we use proper etiquette only when we are with those we don't know, we're simply wearing a mask that sooner or later will fall off to reveal how hypocritical we truly are. So, first and foremost, try to practice good manners with your own family. Never yell at your parents. You can let them know you disagree with something and talk with them about it, but never offend them, laugh at them, or order them around, especially in front of others. (If you feel the need to argue about something, do it later in private.) Don't hurt your siblings by criticizing them in front of your friends or picking on them just for the heck of it.

Ladies and gentlemen of class are not too proud to serve, especially when it takes effort. For example, refilling a pitcher of water during a meal, taking out the trash, keeping their bedrooms tidy, or even taking care of something that may be another's responsibility (making a bed, picking up things scattered all over the house, helping their parents with housework, respecting family schedules, speaking kindly, sacrificing their own plans to babysit their younger siblings, asking if they can help with something). Young children are capable of seeing only their own needs, but some teenagers still behave this way (for example, locking themselves in their room as soon as they get home, going out without letting anyone know where they are, ignoring the rest of the world . . . in short, selfishly thinking the whole solar system revolves around them). You're truly growing and maturing when you begin to notice the needs of others. In sum, if you're not well-mannered in your own home, your good behavior is simply a mask, making a mockery of you.

Conversations

You don't have to like everyone, but if you put others down because of their clothes, the color of their skin, their character, or their ideas, an alert should go off in your head with red lights, blaring sirens, and emergency bells. You've turned into an idiot! Those who think they're better than everyone else will be found out, sooner or later, no matter how hard they try to hide it. So let's get this through our thick skulls: Everyone has something good to offer!

It's better not to ask indiscreet questions, but if it's absolutely necessary, start out with a few words that will soften it such as, "I'm so sorry for asking, but could you tell me . . ."

It's not nice to whisper in someone's ear in front of other people. It makes everyone else uncomfortable because it makes them think you're making fun of them, even if it's not true. It's a great way to make enemies. Tell secrets in private.

If you accidentally say something offensive during a conversation, don't try to fix it by saying you're sorry or justifying yourself (for example, you make a joke about vegetarians and then remember that your mom's friend is a vegetarian. Oops!). Don't try to make up for it by going on and on about the benefits of lettuce, tomato, and carrots. You're sure to make it worse. Just continue naturally with the conversation. Obviously, if the other person is offended, apologize—and if he's really angry, take off running!

If someone reprimands you for a mistake (you bumped into someone, you arrived late, you got distracted while driving), thank the person with a smile. It's hard to do because no one likes to be corrected, but it's a sign of great class. However, if someone corrects you in a rude, insulting, or threatening fashion, let the person know you expect to be treated respectfully. For example, if he or she says, "Look where you're going, stupid!" you could answer, "I apologize! I got distracted, but that's no reason to insult me." If the insults continue, ignore them. You've already said what you had to say, and that person is only making himself or herself look worse.

Bad behavior is very contagious, so avoid risky situations like watching trashy shows, reading cheap magazines (I'm referring to content, not price), or hanging out with a bad crowd. Your own mannerisms and ways of speaking will be affected by these negative influences.

Even though it's easy to do, try not to complement

one person by putting down another (for example, "You drive so well—so much better than your brother. He has such a lead foot.").

It's also wrong to use criticism to praise someone—for example, "Congratulations on the good grades. It's about time you started taking school seriously!" And be careful not to congratulate with a bitter or jealous tone (for example, "Those are really cute pants, Audrey. Of course, since you can afford expensive clothes . . .").

Even though sometimes you might not feel like talking, it's best not to give one-word answers. If someone wants to start a conversation and you're in a hurry, it's OK to say so. If you aren't in the mood to talk about a certain topic, change the subject or simply respond briefly. Sometimes, though, just because we're too lazy to give a decent answer, we can cause others to worry (especially our parents). They could begin thinking to themselves, "Is he in some sort of trouble? Is he sad? Is he upset with us? Is he sick?"—when really it's just that you have something else on your mind (or maybe nothing at all).

Do you truly want to be different and better yourself? Then avoid sexual jokes and swearing in your conversations. I know it's difficult, but this will truly set you apart from the rest, and others will appreciate it in due time. If a conversation among friends about girls (or guys) or about sex seems more appropriate for animals than people (you can usually tell right away because everyone starts laughing and using dirty language), it's best to change the subject or leave. Beautiful things should be treated delicately—and very beautiful things, very delicately.

Avoid swear words, although at times they may be inevitable. The secret is using them as seldom as possible. That way they maintain their force. Those who curse all the time are incapable of showing their anger, disgust, or disdain. If you never use them, then when they become necessary, they will drop like a bomb! It's absolutely ridiculous to think that using four-letter words makes you mature. Save them for intense moments, which are few and far between. Try to notice and remove from your vocabulary expressions such as "that dude," "that chick," "right?" "OK?" "like," etc. These are crutches, expressions that don't add anything to the conversation and serve only to reveal a lazy mind.

Develop good conversational habits. When you speak with people face-to-face, look them in the eye. It shows you're sure of yourself and all of your attention is dedicated to that person. Don't interrupt others when they're talking. As the saying goes, we have one mouth and two ears for a reason, to listen more and speak less. Those who learn this art will be well-liked.

If you must speak or tell someone something, don't go on and on. Every few minutes, pause to ask the other person, "What about you? What do you think?" Those who chatter endlessly exasperate even the deaf! Finally, those who constantly refer back to themselves are annoying: "Well, I think . . ." or "Once I . . ." or "I'm the type of person who . . ." Are you the center of the universe? It happens to me all the time . . . oops!

If you're talking with a group of friends in public—for instance, in a bus or a restaurant—do a volume check every once in a while. Sometimes it seems as if a bunch of Tarzans from different jungles have gotten together to talk about their latest hunt. That doesn't mean you need to whisper (unless you are, in fact, a group of spies sharing top secret information), but keep in mind that if you speak loudly, you can bother others. Because their tone of voice is higher, ladies should be especially careful.

Be aware of the physical aspects of conversation—remember that you're interacting with your body as well as with words. Don't, for example, point your finger at anyone, especially if you're accusing that person of something. It's aggressive, and it looks like you're waving a gun at them.

Nor should you repeatedly touch the arm of someone you're talking to. Don't worry, the person won't disappear if you let go (well, unless you're chatting with Harry Potter or Frodo, who might disappear with a magic cape or a ring). Try to stand at least twenty inches away from those with whom you're speaking (you don't have to measure it out with a ruler; just estimate). That way you won't breathe in their face or invade their space. If you smoke (alas), make sure you keep this in mind.

One of the most disgusting things is smelling someone's bad breath while you're talking to that person. Did you know that in ancient times, the King of Persia ordered his subjects to put their hands in front of their mouths while speaking to him? The odor was so bad that he wanted to avoid smelling it. Even though you're not the King of Persia (if you are, what an honor that you're reading my book!), try to brush your teeth after each meal. If that's not possible, avoid certain foods like onions, fish, and garlic while you're out, or carry breath mints with you. The worst thing is that those who have bad breath tend not to realize it (and they also tend to stand really close to you when they talk). If you're unable to take care of your halitosis (that's what habitual bad breath is called), see your dentist—you may have some type of condition, and it will be really hard to find a boyfriend/girlfriend if you don't get it taken care of!

Speak to others respectfully. Address older people you don't know using "sir" or "ma'am." If you're unsure whether to address them formally or informally, I suggest you begin by addressing them formally. You can use the person's name if he or she invites you to (and by that time, you'll already have made a great impression!). Try to address strangers in the same way (the bus driver, the waiter, etc.) as well as those who have some type of authority over you (the elderly, teachers you don't know very well—yes, I know it's hard to believe, but even your school teachers deserve your respect—priests or ministers, police officers, doctors, too). It's difficult to do if you're not used to it, but it's important that you learn as soon as possible!

Some people use conversation to make themselves feel superior to others. For instance, criticizing others when they're not around has become a common practice. A lady or a gentleman would never do such a thing. Shaming another person to make oneself feel superior is a cowardly act that displays a deep level of insecurity. Using excessive words or expressions from other languages is also a bit ridiculous. "Hey, hermano, I like your jeans, they're super chevere . . . ." Try to avoid such whenever possible.

Greetings

If you're with other young people you don't know, it's OK to introduce yourself using your first name (unless, of course, you are Bond . . . James Bond). If you're introduced to an adult, it's appropriate to say your first and last name, in case they happen to know someone in your family (it's something older people enjoy).

When you're introducing two people who don't know each other, you should introduce the younger person to the older person and the guy to the girl. It's a good idea to include some tidbit to get the conversation started. For example: "Matthew, this is Audrey. Audrey is a really talented actress . . . ."

Shaking hands when you meet someone is truly an art. Did you know that swordsmen were the first to shake hands? When opponents extended their right hands, they knew they weren't going to draw their swords or knives to kill one another in betrayal. It was a noble and peaceful gesture. Therefore, always shake hands with those who initiate the gesture, especially if you happen to carry a sword. To refuse to shake hands is to act like a scoundrel.

A handshake should be tight and firm. While you're shaking hands, look the other person in the eye and smile. It's also appropriate to state your name. Remember, don't shake hands like Jello or like Superman. In other words, don't offer a limp hand (it's very unpleasant to squeeze a weak hand), but don't squeeze so hard you crush someone's fingers, especially if it's an older or weaker person.

A handshake should last an appropriate length of time. You shouldn't let go right away as if the other person were a leper, nor should you hold onto the person's hand as if he or she were going to escape. Two or three seconds are plenty. You can let go after you've both said your names.

Don't shake hands if your palms are sweaty, and don't wipe them on your clothing beforehand. If your hands are dirty or otherwise occupied, excuse yourself by saying something like, "I'm sorry—I would shake your hand, but I've been painting the fence out back." If you're wearing gloves, take them off before shaking hands (unless you're Darth Vader). However, if the other person offers to shake hands with a glove on, don't take yours off so as not to make the person feel bad.

If you're speaking with someone you know, but during the conversation you sense that he or she doesn't remember who you are, try to give hints that might help the person remember you (where you met, mutual friends, etc.). If you're the one who's forgotten the other person's name or the reason you know each other, simply ask (for example, "I'm sorry, of course I remember you, but would you mind telling me your name again?").

If the custom is to greet each other with a kiss on the cheek, as it is for many Europeans, there's no reason to leave the person's face wet, as if you were an octopus or the drooling monster in the movie *Alien*.

Even though it's becoming less and less common, when you call a home phone or a business (in other words, something other than a personal cell phone) or someone you don't know, introduce yourself first and then state the reason for your call. "Good morning, my name is Audrey. Yes, that's right, Audrey Hepburn in the flesh. May I please speak to . . ."

When you enter an enclosed area where only a few people are present (for example, a waiting room or a small store), it's polite to say "good morning" in a moderate tone not directed at anyone in particular. Smile when you're being introduced to someone, even if your favorite football team just lost, you have a terrible toothache, or the screen on your iPhone just broke. There's also an art to saying good-bye. Try to keep it brief. Some people make a big deal out of it, as if the world were coming to an end. It's enough to say good-bye once.

Appointments

Punctuality is one of the defining characteristics of men and women of class. What's the secret? Arrange your schedule so you can arrive five or ten minutes ahead of time. If you're punctual, you're in control of your life, not a slave of time. If for some reason you're running late, call the person who is waiting for you or send a message to indicate whether you'll be a little late, somewhat late, or very late. It's important to be honest. It's disrespectful of the other person's time to say, "I'm almost there," when you're still a half hour away. Sometimes it's embarrassing to tell the truth, but it's always better to bite the bullet than to make your tardiness worse by lying. If you leave a message saying, "I'm so sorry, but I got caught up with something, and I won't be there for another forty minutes because now the traffic is heavy. I apologize," it gives the other person the chance to figure out what to do while he or she waits. And it's especially important if your parents are waiting for you to come home (for example, after a party). At times like these, the number of anxious thoughts that pass through your mother's mind is proportional to the number of minutes that tick by (five minutes: he got distracted; ten minutes: he missed the bus; twenty minutes: he got in a fight; thirty minutes:

he's at a park, drunk; forty-five minutes: he was kid-napped and his kidnappers are deciding on the ransom amount; sixty minutes: someone call the police!). A quick text message or phone call dispels all of these haunting thoughts. It's also important to notify your parents out of respect for them. In summary, do your best to be punctual at all times, let someone know if you'll be late, and apologize when you finally arrive.

Tobacco

You're well aware of what it does to your health, but if you still decide to smoke, it's polite to ask those around you if they mind (especially if children are present). If you're riding in someone else's car, don't ask to use the ashtray unless you know the driver smokes. If you're on a long trip and you start to get jittery, ask the driver if he or she might stop sometime soon so you can have a cigarette.

It's better to go outside to smoke during a meal at a restaurant, but it's preferable to refrain from smoking until after dessert. With the exception of criminal in-terrogations at a police station in the movies, it's also rude to blow smoke in others' faces.

To bum a cigarette off your friends occasionally isn't a big deal. To do it all the time is a good way to lose your friends.

6

POSTURES

Are you familiar with the hunchback of Notre Dame? He was the main character in a book about a deformed man that lived hidden away in the towers of the Cathedral of Paris. His back was so hunched that he could only see only his own two feet, and he had a hump like a camel. I hope the same won't happen to you. Whether you're eating or studying, pay attention to your posture. Try to sit with the lower part of your back resting against the back of the chair. If you need to be closer to your book to see it, it's time to visit the eye doctor. If you need to be closer to your plate to eat, learn how to use silverware.

To walk with class, imagine that someone is gently pulling you by the neck with a string. Don't look at your feet when you walk, but don't stick your nose in the air either—this makes you look as though you feel superior to others. (That's why military personnel wear hats with a large visor. It forces them to lift up their heads to see what's in front of them. That's how they demand respect! If you're in the military, fine; if not, you can relax a little bit).

When you're seated in a formal setting—at church, for instance—don't cross your legs. In other formal settings, such as conferences, it's OK to cross your legs as long as you can do so without showing the bottom of your shoe. When you're at another person's house, remember to maintain good posture. You should be in a comfortable position without transforming from a solid to a liquid state. If you're sitting on the couch watching TV, for instance, don't contort yourself like an octopus. Don't put your feet up on the coffee table or sit on the arm of a chair. Just sit down like a normal human being.

During formal photographs—at weddings, for example—it's best not to cross your arms. Ladies can hold onto their purses with both hands so one arm isn't dangling in the air. During a formal event—i.e., a religious ceremony or a speech—it's not good manners to put your hands in your pockets, unless you happen to be a secret agent who is aiming at someone with a gun hidden under his coat (as James Bond would).

7

MEALS

At the table

One of the best ways to tell if people have good or bad manners is to observe them during meals. Otherwise, just take a look at how your dog eats. Obviously the rules vary a little depending on whether we are at home or at a formal dinner, but I suggest that you follow the most important rules at home as well, even if you're eating alone. That way they'll become natural.

Get used to eating with the center of your back touching the back of the chair. It may be uncomfortable at first if you aren't used to it, but it gets easier over time. If you sit well, you won't pounce on your plate like a starving whale. Huge boa constrictors can sleep for days after eating a large animal. They lean back and nod off. You, on the other hand—unless you're a giant boa—don't need to slide off your chair when you're done eating. In other words, don't lean back in your chair. Try to maintain a comfortable position with your back slightly straight. If you're tired, go sit on the couch once the meal is finished.

When you're seated at the table before the meal is served, unfold your napkin and place it on your lap. During the meal, your hands should always be visible and above your lap. There are a few things you should avoid doing while you're at the table. Don't touch your hair, nose, and ears; don't talk on the phone or answer a text message (if other people do, stare at them until they finish. You'll see how annoying it is!); don't shout at someone at the other end of the table or loudly sing your favorite song (especially if you can't carry a tune!).

If your phone is a point of distraction (because the conversation at the table is boring or you're receiving messages), silence it. Either way, never put it next to your plate or near the food (it's kind of gross because it's been against your ear and may be dirty from being handled). I understand that at some point you may be waiting for that one text message that will change the course of your life and the destiny of all humanity, but you'll be able to eat much more peacefully if you aren't constantly looking at your phone, anxiously waiting to see the message from So-and-So.

If one of the dinner guests suddenly sneezes loudly, continue the conversation without being irritated. It's not necessary to say "Oh my!" or "Goodness gracious!" or "You startled us!" If you're overcome by coughing or sneezing during a meal, try to soften it with a tissue or your napkin. If it doesn't let up, excuse yourself with a hand gesture and leave the room where you can cough or sneeze in peace. When you come back, continue as if nothing happened.

It's polite to wait until all the dinner guests are served before you begin eating. If the meal consists of a hot dish that gets cold very quickly (for example, pasta), it's OK to begin eating. If there are many people at the table, it's enough to wait for those around you to be served.

Perhaps Tarzan would disagree and his monkeys even more so, but it in general it's not appropriate to bite off a piece of bread. It's better to break off pieces with your hands as needed. For goodness sake, don't make little balls with the bread crumbs that fall on the table! Come on, ladies and gents, you aren't in pre-school anymore!

If you're at a formal dinner, steer clear of the following topics for conversation: food (to avoid comparisons), politics (to avoid controversy), religion (because it's not the best place to talk about it) and quantum metaphysical astronomy (because you really have no idea what it is).

When you're dining with several people, it's rude to speak only to those you know or those who are interesting to you and ignore the rest. You should be willing to speak with anyone, and not change seats to sit next to those whose company you enjoy (obviously everyone would want to sit next to Audrey). Ladies and gentlemen of class are able to feel comfortable with whomever they sit next to, even if they're really annoying!

While you're waiting for the food to be brought to the table, it's best not to hog all the dinner rolls and chug all your water. Wait for social cues from others at the table: if they've started on their rolls or salad, you may do so as well. If they're still standing around chatting, you shouldn't dig in just yet. Waiting shows that you have self-control (it goes without saying that you're usually hungry before a meal, but remember, only animals are incapable of controlling their hunger). Don't put your nose in your food to identify the ingredients (that's what my dog does). It's better to ask the cook or the server. If you have a food allergy, let the host or hostess know ahead of time.

If you aren't able to reach something at a large table, avoid contorting your body to do so. Besides bothering those around you, you could also knock down a glass or a bottle. Simply ask the person next to you to pass what you want (saying "please" is a necessity, and it's the magic word for a man or woman of class). Before filling your water glass, check to see if those around you have a full glass. If not, fill their glasses first. But please, don't fill them all the way to the brim, so as not to cause anyone to do a balancing act.

It'ss not polite to use toothpicks in public (it was at one time, but times have changed). If you have food stuck in your teeth and it's bothering you, you can go to the bathroom and take care of it in private.

Eating

It's better not to say "Bon appetit" before eating. Its origin stems from many centuries ago, and it literally means "I hope you burp in satisfaction after the meal," which is not very elegant. Nevertheless, it's so commonly used that if someone else says it to you, simply say "thank you" instead of remaining silent or responding, "I hope you have a great burp, too!"

As you well know, don't chew with your mouth open or talk with your mouth full. If someone asks you a question while you're chewing, don't answer until you have swallowed your food. Take your time. It's also not polite to clean your plate with a piece of bread, unless you're with family, even if you spear the bread with a fork.

Don't add salt to your food when you're eating at someone else's house, so as not to offend the person who made the meal (although it's OK when you're at a restaurant). If the person who cooked the meal offers you salt, you may accept it.

It's not polite to blow on your food to cool it off. It's better to wait a few minutes and take small bites to make it cool off faster.

I suggest not filling your soup spoon to the brim. If you do, it's likely to spill over when you bring it toward your mouth, causing the soup to drip on you. A simple trick is to touch the base of the spoon to the interior lip of the bowl. That way, you'll eliminate the drop that forms underneath the spoon. If the soup is served in a bowl with handles, it's OK drink the last little bit directly from the bowl without using a spoon.

Before drinking, clean your mouth with a napkin. That way, you'll avoid getting the brim of the glass dirty from the food on your lips. This is difficult to re-member to do. If you start doing it at home, little by little it will become a habit. If necessary, clean your mouth again after you have taken a drink—for exam-ple if you've had milk (yes, even secret agents drink milk behind closed doors) or if you've gotten a few drops on your lips.

Is it OK to have seconds at someone else's house? Yes, that's not a problem. It's actually good manners if you've been invited to lunch or dinner, but wait until more food is offered to you. If you ask for seconds and there isn't any food left, you'll make the host/hostess feel bad. If you don't care for a second helping when it's offered, it's classy to say, "No thank you, but it was delicious" or something similar. Avoid expressions like "Seriously, I'm about to explode!" unless you're among close friends in an informal setting.

Pasta noodles can sometimes be an issue. You should only coil them up with your fork, never cut them with a knife. You may need to twist the fork around several times until you're able to get a portion small enough to fit in your mouth. Make sure you don't make a huge ball of pasta that you can't swallow. Try to avoid noodles hanging off your fork because then you'll have to slurp them up, causing a rain shower of tomato sauce. It's also impolite to bite the pasta off with your teeth. As you can see, eating pasta is an art. Be patient with yourself, and good luck!

Vegetables and omelets should be cut with a fork only. Dried fruit and olives are eaten with your hands (of course, you shouldn't break the dried fruit with your fist or your teeth because you'll end up breaking the fruit, your fist, and your teeth at the same time). You can deposit the olives pits and the seeds of oranges, grapes, and other fruits right into your hand and then place them discreetly on your plate. You may also eat pizza with your hands, even at a restaurant. Chicken should be eaten with silverware, unless you're eating wings.

You shouldn't leave anything on your plate at the end of the meal (except bones and peels). It's rude to leave a substantial portion of food, because the host might think you didn't like it. If that's the case or you served yourself too much, finish it anyway. Leaving a bite or two is considered polite in some parts of the world and is not considered rude in most places, especially if you make sure to compliment the cook on the food.

You should touch your glass only when you're drinking from it or making a toast; don't play around with it. Don't drink with both hands, and don't get up from the table to fill your glass.

Even though it may be a common custom, it isn't necessary to clink glasses when you make a toast. It's enough to raise your glass toward the person you're toasting. If everyone else clinks glasses, you may follow suit, but limit it to the guests who are seated right next to you. If you're asked to make a toast, the proper way to do it is to stand up, raise your glass, and make a brief toast, not go on and on. The message should always be positive and joyful. If you have an inkling that you'll be asked to make a toast (because it's your birthday or another special occasion), try to have an idea what you're going to say ahead of time.

Silverware

Learning to use silverware properly assists you to maneuver your food without leaning over your plate to eat (as dogs and cats do). Maintaining an upright position is a talent, especially if you're eating soup or a plate of pasta, but it's a sign of great class. You should hold your silverware by the stem, not closer to where the food is. The fork is held straight up, not grabbed. In other words, don't wield it like a knife—hold it like a pen. Use your steak knife to cut your meat, not pull it apart. If your knife isn't sharp, simply have a little patience or ask for another one, but either way, don't become frustrated and start stabbing the meat (which is obviously already dead; if it starts moving, let the waiter know right away).

Never put your knife in your mouth, only your fork, soup spoon, and teaspoon. When you prepare a piece of food to put in your mouth, make sure it's not too big. If it is, you may look like the raging lion from Metro Goldwin Mayer. If you see that the portion is too big as you lift it off the plate, rectify the situation naturally. Simply place your fork back on your plate and cut a smaller portion. If you're eating a piece of meat or fish that needs to be cut, do it as you go along: Cut a piece and eat it, then cut another piece and eat it. Don't cut the whole piece at once (unless you're cutting meat for children).

Eating fruit with silverware is not easy, but you should learn to do so because sooner or later you'll find yourself in a situation where it's necessary. Peeling oranges with a knife and fork is quite difficult, whereas cantaloupe is easy. Eat bananas with a fork only; don't cut them with a knife. You may eat plums, mandarins, peaches, and grapes with your hands.

If you drink coffee, don't leave the spoon inside the cup. It's not good manners, and besides, you could end up blind in one eye. The spoon belongs on the right side of the saucer. It's best to leave your silverware on your plate while you're drinking or taking a bite. If you haven't finished, place your silverware a couple inches apart (as if it were the hands on a clock indicating 4:40). If you're finished, place your silverware together vertically (as if it were 6:30). The servers recognize these signals and will know if they should take your plate or not.

If you're at a formal dinner where there are several pieces of silverware, begin by using those farthest from the plate. The place setting tends to look like this: The forks are at the left of the plate and the spoon and knives to the right (for meat or fish). The silverware needed for dessert is found at the head of the plate. The fish knife, which is typically a palette knife, is not used to cut the fish but rather to separate it into pieces and place them on your fork. (Fish is usually much softer than meat.)

At the end of a meal

It's not polite to get up from the table until everyone has finished. If you must leave, excuse yourself first. If you've been invited to someone's home, say "thank you" once again at the end of the gathering or send a message the next day (even if it's a text message). If you're at a restaurant, leave your napkin unfolded next to your plate at the end of the meal.

It's both polite and expected to leave a tip at a restaurant unless the establishment specifically indicates otherwise. If you're a poor university student, you won't be able to leave a fortune, but you should try to leave something. At a bar, you can leave the change for the bartender. It's an extra gesture of kindness to the waiter or waitress to tip in cash rather than on your credit or debit card. But be careful when you travel! In some countries you can actually offend the waiter if you tip them. Be sure you know the customs beforehand.

8

HYGIENE

At twelve or thirteen years of age, our body glands change. Our sweat begins to have an odor, and our bodies produce more oil. The issue is that sometimes adolescents don't notice it, but others do. It's important to be attentive to these changes so you can adapt your hygiene habits to your age. This is one of the best ways to show self-respect and respect toward others. Besides, you'll be much more comfortable.

You should take a shower every day, preferably in the morning. Although it may be difficult to get up earlier, it will wake you up and wash off the previous night's sweat. Taking a shower doesn't mean merely getting wet—you have to use soap. If you have short hair, you can wash it every day (no one goes bald from shampooing). If you have long hair, whether you're a guy or a girl, you may not be able to wash it every day, but make sure it's clean. If you have a particular issue—such as greasy hair or dandruff—there are special shampoos you can use. After you shower, remove the hair that has fallen into the drain using a wad of toilet paper. It's much more pleasant for those who shower after you not to find a jungle inside.

Apply deodorant under your arms every day after showering. In the summer it may be necessary to re-apply it more than once throughout the day. Perfume or cologne should have a subtle scent. Don't douse yourself with tons of cologne or waste half a bottle of your mom's perfume, even if it's a special day. If you use these products daily with moderation, you'll achieve just the right personal touch. Girls tend to be much more concerned about everything related to cosmetics. But because they use more products than guys (soap, shampoo, lotions, makeup, lipstick, and so on), they should be very careful to combine any fragrances well in order to achieve a pleasant scent that goes along with their personality and the circumstances.

One of the greatest mysteries of the universe is why some people (usually guys) aren't able to smell their stinky shoes, even when they smell as if they were made out of whale skin! Just in case, ask your mom or a close friend to let you know when the first hint of smelliness arises. In order to avoid this problem, you can take several precautions: get new shoes if nec-essary; use anti-odor insoles, which are sold at most pharmacies; use an antifungal cream if fungus is the cause of the odor; place sweaty shoes out in the sun to dry (if they remain moist, they become atomic bombs). If you have to put your sweaty shoes in a bag after an athletic event, fill the bag with newspaper to absorb some of the moisture.

Take good care of your skin and hands. Pimples are a normal part of adolescence and develop under certain circumstances (like stress). They shouldn't be a reason for embarrassment. Wash your face frequently and be patient. If you have many pimples (acne), however, it's best to consult a dermatologist.

One of the most revealing parts of a person is the hands. It's well worth it to take care of them. Guys, don't let your fingernails grow too long, but make sure they're clean if they're a bit long. Don't bite your nails or hangnails. See a doctor if you have warts. Clean off any pen marks, and of course make sure you clean underneath your fingernails!

Monkeys pick their noses with great pleasure; people don't—or shouldn't. Sometimes people truly appear as if they're drilling for oil. It's better not to do it at all, even when you're alone, because you could do it without realizing it in a public place. If it becomes necessary, use a tissue (as you can see, tissues are great allies to ladies and gentlemen of class).

When you go to the bathroom, it's not necessary to

specify why you're going there ("I've gotta go . . ."). Simply say, "I'll be back in a minute." For guys, when you relieve yourself, be conscientious enough to lift both the top and the seat of the toilet seat (in your own home as well). The next person who may need to sit on it will appreciate this kind gesture. That way, you'll avoid leaving drops of urine on the seat. (There will always be some drops—no one is Robin Hood while going to the bathroom.) When you're finished, always flush the toilet (yes, even if you're only urinating). If you finish a roll of toilet paper, it's good manners to take the time to put on a new roll, if one is available, and throw the empty cardboard tube in the trash.

Even though the bathroom is an intimate place and one where we often struggle with our own self-image, we must respect the urgent needs of others. If someone tries to open the door while you're inside, hurry and finish as quickly as possible, and return later if necessary. The attitude of "I'm in here, and I'll stay here until I'm finished" could cause a tragedy on the other side of the door.

The elegant Audrey would never go to the bathroom with her friends. She could be found in conversation over a cup of tea, taking a stroll through the park, trying on sunglasses, or window shopping, but never going on an outing to the bathroom with other women. It's simply not refined.

Mustaches, goatees, sideburns, and beards are all acceptable ways to create your own image and express your personality, but avoid looking unkempt. Even what some call the "three-day shadow" requires a certain amount of upkeep (by shaving the random hairs that pop up on your cheeks and neck). If you don't trim the edges of your mustache, don't comb your hair, or if you look like a Christmas tree with newly fallen snow because you have so much dandruff, you're letting yourself go. Each person has his or her own personal style, but one of the differences between animals and human beings is that animals don't take care of themselves. So, take care of yourself.

After you've brushed your teeth, washed your face, or cut your nails, rinse the sink clean with a little bit of water. If you have a retainer or braces, avoid taking the retainer out in public or playing around with the rubber bands in your braces in front of others. It's also a good idea to take a quick look in the mirror after each meal to make sure no food has gotten stuck (a piece of lettuce or broccoli, for instance).

9

CLOTHING

The way you dress reflects who you are. Therefore, when you dress, you should be comfortable while at the same time protecting your dignity. To dress with elegance boosts your self-esteem. Wearing a shirt without stains, a pair of pants that fits properly, and a jacket that smells clean will make you feel comfortable. Brand names can assure you of good quality, but avoid trying to look like a fashion model.

It's good to follow styles trends as long as they're not ridiculous. Letting your pants fall down so others can see what brand of underwear you're wearing is very ill-mannered. The same goes for women who wear excessively high heels. If you like extremes in fashion, take a look at pictures of those who wore "the latest fashions" in the 1970s, 80s, and 90s. You'll get a kick out of it!

It's better not to dress like celebrities. They are VIPs, and you are you. A famous person who dresses like trash will be looked upon as eccentric and alternative, but if you dress like trash, you'll look like trash. If you have stains on your clothes, it looks like you're lazy and don't care about your appearance. Change as soon as possible.

If you're wearing tennis shoes (even though dress shoes are always more elegant), at least make sure they're clean and not all sweaty (and make sure they don't smell!). You should wear only white socks with tennis shoes.

Make sure you're well-informed before going to a formal event. There's a big difference between daytime and nighttime events, an academic celebration and a gala dinner, a wedding and a funeral. For ladies, the best option is to have a little black dress that fits you well and lots of accessories (or lots of friends with accessories). The motto of elegance is "less is more." The same goes for your shoes and hairstyle. They should reflect the image you wish to portray and be appropriate to the occasion. There's an old adage that never fails: Whatever you're wearing should allow you to move about freely and act with elegance. Just like Audrey, of course. If your feet hurt terribly, your hairpins are falling out, and your bangs are all over the place, you'll never win.

Excessively tight clothing, dresses with a low neck-line, very short skirts, and gaudy colors are not elegant.

They might even distract others from concentrating on your intelligence, your sense of humor, and your conversation. If you use other methods to attract attention (although these may require more patience), such as kindness, interesting conversation, a good sense of humor, or consistency, you'll win the hearts of guys who are really worth it. Let's get one thing straight: It's nice to be noticed. But don't let your external appearance distract others from seeing the real you.

Don't touch up your makeup in public or in other situations that require your full attention (when you're driving, for instance). Your makeup should correspond to the way you're dressed, the circumstances, the place, and even the time of day. Ask the makeup experts at the department store if you have any questions.

When you're shopping for clothes, don't enter a dressing room with other people. Ask them to wait outside and call them in once you're ready so they can give their opinion on how you look. Try to dress according to current fashions, but don't let fashion dress you. In other words, you should be proud of what you see in the mirror. Stay away from extremes. Dressing well should be important to you, but it should not be the be-all and end-all. Appearances are important, but they're not everything.

I would like to quote some words from Audrey Hepburn (yes, her—the one and only!), who shared some of her favorite beauty tips:

> For attractive lips, speak words of kindness. For lovely eyes, seek out the good in people. For a slim figure, share your food with the hungry. For beautiful hair, let a child run his fingers through it once a day. For poise, walk with the knowledge that you never walk alone. . . . The beauty of a woman is not in the clothes she wears, the figure that she carries, or the way she combs her hair. The beauty of a woman is seen in her eyes, because that is the doorway to her heart, the place where love resides. True beauty in a woman is reflected in her soul. It's the caring that she lovingly gives, the passion that she shows and the beauty of a woman only grows with passing years.

Isn't that magnificent?

For gentlemen dressing for special occasions, a classic style is to wear shoes and a belt of the same color—both black or both brown—black socks, a long-sleeved dress shirt, and a tie with a medium-sized knot (not too big and not too small). If it's a dinner gala or a wedding, the best way to dress up is still a suit and tie. Make sure your tie is snug at your neck (you shouldn't be able to see the top button of your shirt) and straight. There are plenty of apps that can show you how to tie a necktie properly—there are over ninety ways to make a knot. The one that is widest is the easiest to tie. You'll look like you're half a Windsor, but a very elegant one at that. Look for it on YouTube. Your tie should match your shirt and jacket, just as your belt should match your shoes, so choose colors that go well together. Jeans give an informal touch to a jacket and tie. This combination is not the best option, but if they're a nice, clean pair, jeans can work in certain settings.

It's better for men not to overdo it on accessories (rings, chains, bracelets, etc.). If you want to be noticed, wear a snazzy watch. Make sure it matches the rest of what you're wearing (and if you're going with Frodo, make sure you have "the" ring!). You should use sunglasses only when you're outside in the sunshine. If you're inside or in the shade, take them off. Otherwise, it just looks like you're looking for attention. (On the other hand, if attention is precisely what you want, go ahead and keep them on, but watch out for the stairs!). It's also good manners to take off your sunglasses when you run into people you know while you're out so they can look you in the eyes while you're talking.

Make sure the clothes you wear are appropriate for the environment and the activity. Your clothing is an important factor for your self-esteem. If you wear clothes that are too informal for the occasion, you won't be taken seriously, and you'll feel uncomfortable and out of place. Remember: Your clothes are important when making a first impression, and you have only one chance to make a good first impression.

10

NEW TECHNOLOGIES

Smartphones

As a general rule, avoid making phone calls before 9:00 AM, after 9:00 PM, and during meals. If the person you've called seems busy, politely ask the person if he or she is free to talk or if it would be better to call back later. If the person says, "Could you call me back later?" don't continue the conversation with something like, "Oh, OK. I was just calling to tell you . . ." No! Call back later!

Don't answer the phone or make calls in inappropriate places (such as a public bathroom). Make a habit of putting your phone on mute during classes, at hospitals, religious ceremonies, dinners, restaurants, museums, concerts, movies, and theaters. Turning off the ringer shows great respect toward the place you're entering or the person you're visiting. Don't put your cell phone on the table while you're eating. It's something you hold up to your ear, and it could be dirty. Besides, it could be bothersome to others at the table if you haven't muted your phone and it rings while you're eating.

It has become more and more commonplace to use cell phones when we're with others to surf the web, chat, or look up information. Try to avoid using your phone as an escape. Interpersonal relationships suffer if you don't make an effort during a boring moment or when you run out of things to talk about (such as when you're out on a date, hanging out with your friends, or traveling with your parents). At times like these "force yourself" to be attentive to those around you.

If you're waiting for an important phone call while you're at dinner or at your friend's house, it's best to let them know ahead of time and then excuse yourself when you have to leave to take the call. If you aren't the First Lady or the President of the United States—and something tells me you're not—there's no reason to be on your phone every second while you're at the movies or McDonald's. Those who are give the impression that they're bored, and that's not an appealing impression to give.

Try to keep your conversations brief and speak in a moderate tone if you're in an enclosed area (bus, train, store, subway). It's true that everyone does it, but that doesn't mean it's the best idea. Some people talk so loudly on the phone, it's as if they were shouting to the satellite. It isn't necessary to raise your voice! Either way, always avoid private conversations when you're out in public—don't discuss friends, teachers, girls or guys, the secret plans of the enemy to attack the Queen of England, and so on. If the person you're talking with goes on and on and you want to get off the phone, you could tell a little white lie (in other words, a lie that doesn't harm anyone). For example, you could say, "I'm sorry I'm going to have to let you go, but I have something I have to do. Would you like me to call you again later?"

Your ringtone reflects your personal character. But even though you may enjoy listening to bugle calls, the resounding band Psychosis, or heavy metal, you're not the only one that will be hearing it. Consider this: If you receive a call when there are other people around and you have to hurry up and turn off the sound, perhaps it's a sign it's time to change your ringtone.

If you receive a call from a number you don't recognize or a private number, you should answer "Yes?" or "Hello?" instead of a threatening "Who is it?" If a call is dropped, the person who made the phone call initially should be the one to call back.

Headphones

Using headphones to listen to music is wonderful, but you should take them off—yes, both sides—when you're dealing with others, even if you don't think it will be necessary to talk (for instance, when you're checking out at the grocery store, paying the bus driver, or saying hello to your mother when you get home). These people will be thankful that, if they have to tell you something, they won't have to repeat themselves. It's not enough to turn off the music; the other person can't tell if it's on or off. The polite thing to do is remove your headphones.

Listening to loud music on your headphones in enclosed places can be very annoying to others (subway, bus, waiting room). Not everyone enjoys hip hop, heavy metal, or rap!

Communicating electronically

Avoid sending messages in all capital letters. It's just as annoying as someone yelling into your ear! Keep abbreviations to a minimum when writing messages. Everyone appreciates when someone has taken the time to write well. Make a habit of rereading your messages after you write an email or text. It reduces the possibility of making grammatical or punctuation errors. Your messages give a glimpse of your character and reveal your personality much more than you may think.

Make the effort to answer all messages that require confirmation, even if just briefly. Those who don't take the time to do this appear arrogant. For example, "James Bond, this is Audrey. Can you come and rescue me? . . . James, please . . . James? . . ." If you have to cancel an appointment, it's best to call the person by phone. Sending a text message is a bit blunt and somewhat cowardly.

Don't send emails or text messages with inappropriate or unnecessary photos or videos (i.e., all the selfies you took with your friends at Saturday night's concert). If the other person doesn't have a good Internet connection, you could clog his or her inbox or use up all the data on the person's phone. And don't forward chain emails. The Earth is not going to explode; you won't be the victim of bad luck; and unfortunately, you won't save a child in a third-world country. You'll simply fill your friends' inboxes with useless messages while simultaneously revealing your electronic naivety.

If you're sending an email to several people at once, send it by blind copy (BCC). That way, if those receiving it don't already know each other, they won't be able to see the other email addresses. An email account is personal and should not be given out to just anyone, especially if it's someone else's email address.

Facebook

Don't tag a friend with photos on *Facebook* or *Snapchat* if you think they may not like it; the picture might not have turned out well or you may have caught them in a ridiculous situation). When in doubt, it's best not to identify them.

We all have a "virtual life" that begins earlier and earlier and lasts our entire life. Therefore, choose well how you portray yourself in emails and social media. It's best to use your real name. Nicknames end up coming back to haunt you later (for example, jamesthepig. com or audreysupertop@gmail.com are email addresses that won't last long).

Who doesn't love to receive a personal greeting on one's birthday? If it's just an acquaintance, a message on *Facebook* is sufficient, but if it's a close friend or a relative, a message on *Facebook* isn't enough. If you aren't able to see the person that day, it's always better to call him or her over the phone. And don't forget sending a real birthday card through the postal service!

It's not tasteful to publish or share obscene or vulgar images. Bad taste is contagious, and you should also consider the long-term consequences. Imagine that you've spent years building up a good reputation only to have it come crashing down in a matter of minutes because someone (your children, your boss) sees what you shared on Facebook one crazy Sunday afternoon when you were a teenager.

Text messaging

A conversation with someone who is right in front of you is always more important than texting. It shows great self-control if you don't immediately look at your phone when you get a message while you're with someone else. The majority of people, like Pavlov's dog, just can't resist. (If you don't know who Pavlov's dog is, you can Google it.) When you control yourself and read your message later, it communicates clearly to the person you're with: "I'm in control of my life, and right now I'm paying attention to you."

It's not a good idea to talk to a friend while you're texting with someone else at the same time. You could simply say, "Give me just a minute while I finish up this text, and I'll be right with you." That way you can give both friends your full attention.

Before texting a joke or a phrase that can have two meanings (or posting something you think could hurt someone's feelings on Facebook), read it over two or three times. If you still aren't sure, don't send it right away. Wait a few minutes, then read it again. Do the same thing if you're answering someone you're arguing with and things are getting more heated. Because you're not able to see body language or hear tones of voice, texting can create misunderstandings and upset people. It's often best to stop texting and call the other person.

If you're part of a group text and two people begin a side conversation among themselves, it's best if they break off and start a new conversation by themselves instead of boring everyone else with unwanted messages.

Text alerts can be irritating to those around you. If you're having a conversation in a public place, silence the alerts. Sometimes it's difficult to end a text message conversation. The conversation goes on and on, but you don't know how to cut it off without being rude. Simply wrap it up with an pleasant but clear message that lets the other person know you have to go. For example, you could say, "Well, I have to go study now. See you soon!"

11

GUYS AND GALS

Male and female friends

Everyone knows that men and women are different. Neither men nor women are better or worse than the other; we are simply different. (That's why we are attracted to each other! Men possess qualities women lack and vice versa. We mutually complement and better each other.) Therefore, always treat the opposite sex with respect and admiration because you can learn a lot from them.

In general, girls are more in tune with their feelings (emotions) and guys with tangible experiences. It's a small difference, but that's the way it is. This difference attracts us to each other and helps us to discover that we are incomplete beings. But because guys are more in tune with "experience," if you sit on their laps, or wrestle with them, or make some kind of physical contact with them—a hug, a little shove, etc.—it's very likely that a guy will interpret the gestures differently than a girl would.

In general (but not always), guys are tougher and more solid physically and less sensitive emotionally than girls. Guys, you can push your guy friend, greet him with a slap upside the head, or throw a ball at him really hard, but you shouldn't do these things to girls! Of course you can joke around with girls, but you have to be more mindful. It's best to avoid joking about their clothes, their weight, their physical appearance, their sexual relations, and their feelings out of respect and in order to avoid doing unimaginable long-term damage.

Even though, thanks be to God, times have changed, guys should treat girls with chivalrous details that are still appreciated: pull their chair back for them, open the door for them, compliment them on their new outfit or hairstyle, and so on. But of course, this doesn't give girls the liberty to turn the guys into their personal "servants."

Guys: If you're talking about something and suddenly a girl begins to cry, don't look for a way to escape. Hang in there. At times like these, the best way to help is simply to listen and be there for her. Who knows, you may need to vent with her some other time.

I advise you to talk about your deepest issues (your love life, your family, your health) with only your very closest friends. Don't tell your problems to the whole world.

When you're going up or down a narrow staircase, the guy should always go ahead of the girl, in order to clear the path for the girl when going up or prevent a possible fall when going down (guys tend to be bigger, so if they trip they will cause greater damage). It's a gentlemanly gesture, just like opening a car door for a girl, pulling back her chair for her, letting her walk through the door first, or ordering the pizza and bringing it to the table. Old-fashioned? No, these details aren't old-fashioned. They're classy. If a guy can do them naturally, all the better.

It's impolite to follow a girl with your eyes, and it's offensive to do so rudely. You're acting like an animal if you refer to one of her physical characteristics or whistle catcalls or start howling like a Neanderthal. If you notice that one of your friends can't control himself, suggest that he go to the butcher shop and drool all over the meat on display.

Another way to be one of a kind is not to criticize anyone. Sometimes it's enough for a classmate of ours to pass by for them to become the target of all our poisonous arrows. Let's face it, we all like to gossip. Unfortunately, throwing another person under the bus makes us feel superior to him or her. Nevertheless, it's a sign of immaturity. Hopefully, you'd rather imitate Robin Hood and defend the poor (poor in character, elegance, friendships), asking others not to criticize them behind their backs. Defend them by helping their good qualities shine through. Even though you may be alone in your efforts, those who are listening will realize that when there not around and someone is criticizing them, you'll come to their defense.

If you invite friends over to your house, call your mom or dad to let them know ahead of time, especially if they're going to stay for lunch or dinner or are planning to spend the night. Perhaps it's not a good day for them, or there might be a family issue you're not aware of. Of course, when you invite others over, you have certain obligations. Make sure your guests are comfortable, let them know where the bathrooms are, and don't leave them alone for long periods of time. If forgetting your iPhone is a big deal, forgetting about your friends is an even bigger deal!

Girlfriends and boyfriends

Pet names between boyfriends and girlfriends should be saved for intimate moments when you're alone. If you're around others, even if you're among friends, you should use given names. "Babe," "Honey," "Teddy Bear," "Princess," and similar pet names sound ridiculous to others (and to the couple, too, but we all know that love is deaf and blind).

Avoid showing intimate displays of affection in public (caressing, hugging, kissing), especially in front of your friends. Even if those who see you don't know you, these moments are no longer intimate if they're done in the middle of the street. Being alone makes intimate moments your own, and they're best kept between the two of you.

A classy courtship knows how to respect boundaries. Until you have publicly declared that you want to share your life with this person, his or her intimacy does not belong to you, and you must respect it. Think about your future life. What would happen if you bumped into the person five years from now? Would you be able to look him or her in the eye without remorse? If you show each other mutual respect and decide to embark on a chaste journey together, you can be sure that you'll be able to give that person what you have not given to anyone else—the deepest part of you.

If you think it's time to break up with your boyfriend or girlfriend, think about how you're going to explain your reasons. Avoid improvising, because you can end up saying hurtful things. Let the person know the reasons without offending him or her. If you need to take a break for a while, say that, but if you're sure it's time to break up for good, don't create false hopes. Look for a quiet place to have the conversation where you can talk without interruptions. Don't break up over the phone or by texting or in front of others. If the other person is really hurt and begins speaking ill of you, it's best to remain silent and not defend yourself by telling your version of the story. After a breakup, always speak well of the other person, without sharing the details of what didn't work out.

Remember that if you're driving somewhere on a first formal date, it's gentlemanly to open and close the car door for the girl. She will surely thank you for the chivalrous act. Obviously, you should do the same if you're traveling with an older person or someone with physical limitations. Agent 007, after fighting the enemy on his most recent mission, would use his last bit of strength to open the door of his convertible for the magnificent *Audrey*.

If you want to do something special and give someone a bouquet of flowers (your date, your mother, your aunt, for instance), make sure you tell the florist the reason for the flowers (and how much you're willing to spend if you have a tight budget). Every flower has a different meaning, and you wouldn't want to stick your foot in your mouth. For example, red roses symbolize love, while yellow roses symbolize friendship. Bouquets should be different, depending on whether you're giving one to your girlfriend, a friend who just had a baby, your grandmother for her birthday, or a family who just lost a loved one.

12

SPORTS

While playing sports, our competitive spirit reaches its highest level and drives our passion, which is something we need to compete. But sometimes our instincts take over and begin to control our actions. For example, if someone kicks us while we are playing soccer, our self-defense instinct drives us to react immediately. However, if you keep your cool during these extreme moments, the great gentleman or lady inside of you will shine through to others and will make sure you don't allow yourself to be carried away by the heat of the moment.

Follow the rules of each sport. Limitations are imposed precisely to make the sport more fun and challenging. If your opponents aren't respecting the rules, let them know you notice, but don't waste your energy calling them out on every single infraction. Sometimes you win by losing.

When you help an opponent when he falls down, it brings humanity back to the sport. Say you're sorry when necessary. Don't get angry when someone hurts you and then fails to apologize. Be patient. Everyone at one time or another encounters people who act as if they were a descendent of King Kong.

No matter what may have happened during the game, it's always classy to shake hands with members of the opposing team when it's finished. To refuse is to make yourself the bad guy. If you're playing a sport with a ball and you accidentally throw it way off course or another person throws it in your direction, it's good sports etiquette to go after it.

Complaining out loud, criticizing other members of the team, or making excuses when the game goes south shows very little class. You show great self-control when you manage to maintain a positive tone or keep your mouth shut. The same goes when you're watching a game on TV.

If you win a game, even if you're playing with friends, it's not good to rub the loss in their face with nasty comments and jokes. You won, and that's that.

13

SITUATIONS

On public transportation

If the bus is extremely full, take off your backpack (if you have one) as you get on and keep your arms close to your body in order to get through the crowd without bumping into people. Say, "Excuse me," and if you need to push a bit to get in, do so slowly, asking people's pardon (it shouldn't be like a stampede of crazy elephants!) Try to remain calm. These are certainly uncomfortable situations for everyone. It's better to miss the bus and have to walk a little bit than to break a defenseless elderly woman's foot who could turn out to be Agent 008, the national judo champion with a black belt in karate.

If you have a backpack or a handbag, don't place it on the seat next to you unless the bus is fairly empty. If someone indicates that he or she wants to sit there, don't roll your eyes and sigh as if to say, "Oh, excuuuuse me!" It's bad manners to put your feet up on the seat in front of you. Yes, I know it's much more comfortable, but you're not in your living room.

As you already know, it's classy to give up your seat for older people, pregnant women, or women with small children. If you're in doubt about whether or not to offer certain persons your seat (because they're at an age where they could either be grateful for the gesture or offended that you consider them old), it's enough to get up from your seat and leave it open. Those around you will understand that you've left it open for them. If some smart aleck takes your seat, be patient. He's simply making himself look bad in front of everyone.

Avoid talking on the phone on the bus, the subway, the train, or other forms of public transportation. If it becomes necessary, speak in a moderate tone and for the least amount of time possible. If you're traveling with friends on public transit, make sure your conversations are positive. It can be disturbing to others, especially to children, to hear you criticize your teacher, speak ill of a classmate, or talk about last Saturday's game using foul language. Change the subject or say something positive.

If you're listening to music with headphones, make sure it's not loud enough for others to hear it. Public transit vehicles are enclosed and very noisy. The person seated next to you could have a headache or be dealing with family problems. Who knows? He could even be a psychopathic assassin who goes crazy when he hears music!

Pay attention to your movements when you're carrying a bag or backpack in a public place. Try not to be like an adolescent elephant that's having trouble getting used to the size of its own body and is continually bumping into things or throwing things. If someone bumps into you, it probably won't affect you any more than if a fly were to land on your head, but if you bump into a ninety-year-old woman, you could dislocate her shoulder.

If you're on an escalator, remain on the right side if you don't intend to walk up so as not to block it off for those behind you, especially if you're with a group of friends. People might be running late for their appointments or about to miss their flight or may have another emergency. Don't get annoyed if someone asks to pass you, and ask nicely if you need to pass someone.

At funerals

Unfortunately, sooner or later we will experience the death of someone close to us. It's OK to cry, but you should have your emotions in check, without letting yourself get overwhelmed by them. It may help someone else to see you calm.

At a funeral it's proper to express your condolences

to the family of the deceased in a simple fashion. Something like "I'm so sorry for your loss" or "I'll keep him or her in my prayers" is appropriate. Men should attend a funeral with dark pants and a white dress shirt. It's not necessary to wear a black tie. Women should wear dressy, dark clothes, but obviously not a festive party dress.

If a religious ceremony has already begun, it's best to wait until it has finished before greeting the rest of those in attendance. Quite often many family friends know each other, and greetings can turn into a madhouse right in front of the deceased, which can be very disagreeable to close family members.

If you're a close friend or family member of those affected very deeply by the death and are accompanying them, it's good manners to be very attentive by way of supporting them in every way possible. If waiting periods occur between ceremonies (a burial tends to progress slowly), some people prefer to remain silent, while others are grateful if we distract them by talking about something else (make sure it's something appropriate. It wouldn't be right to talk about football or fashion or to start telling jokes). Still others may ask us to pray with them, or they may want to share their favorite memories of the person who passed away. You'll have to adapt to the situation depending on those you're with. You can be the one to strike up a conversation if you see someone who's alone, but be sensitive to whether or not the person wants to talk.

If you receive the news that a relative or close friend of someone very dear to you has died, such as your best friend's father, you can call the person by phone to express your condolences when you think a sufficient amount of time has passed (in other words, wait a few hours instead of calling immediately). If you not sure if it's a good time, you can send them a message saying, "I heard the news—I'm so sorry. May I call you?" It's a good idea to think about what you're going to say ahead of time (you should primarily express sentiments of consolation and encouragement). If you're not very close to the person, you can send a text message with your condolences and a positive comment about the person who has passed away ("We were fortunate to have known him. Now we'll be able to call on him for help from heaven," or something similar).

At the library

A public library is a place to read and study; therefore, it should be relatively quiet. When you first get there, it's sometimes difficult to adapt to the silence right away, and you may run the risk of walking in like an elephant in a porcelain shop (slamming the door, dragging your chair, throwing your wallet and books on the table with a thud, saying hello to everyone, inhaling sharply when someone cute passes by, etc). Avoid these kinds of triumphant entries.

If you're getting up or sitting down while in a silent atmosphere, try to balance your weight so you don't drag the chair on the floor. You should push it away from the table or pull it toward the table by lifting it slightly off the floor, not by dragging it. It requires a little more effort, but it's classier.

Studying while listening to music is a joke. Your brain can't pay attention to two things at once. Well, it can, but not very well. Those who say theirs can (unless they're doing something that doesn't require much thought, like drawing) are either kidding themselves or are aliens with two brains. (Don't trust such people. They could be trying to kidnap you.) Besides, in a quiet atmosphere, it can bother those who are truly trying to use their brains to concentrate on just one thing. If you need help, it's normal to ask a classmate for things like borrowing their notes or quizzing each other to study, but to ask every day is over the top.

At parties

If you're invited to a party, RSVP to let the host know whether you're planning to attend or not. To show up at a party where you're not invited is bad manners. If you bring a friend to a party when only you were invited, ask the person who invited you ahead of time. For example, you might say, "Hello Audrey, my cousins are in town visiting. Would it be OK if they came to the party with me?").

Even though parties usually have a pretty flexible schedule, try to arrive close to the time they're due to start. The host or hostess likes everyone to have a good time from the very beginning. If the party is celebrating someone's birthday or anniversary, don't show up empty-handed. Bring a thoughtful gift of some kind. If you get stuck, a book, a CD, a box of chocolates, or a movie are always well received.

Eat and drink moderately. If you're really hungry, try not to monopolize the sandwiches. One way of controlling yourself is to offer to go around with the tray of appetizers or the wine bottle to serve others. When everyone else has had enough, you can eat more calmly. Don't rush to get something to eat and drink. My advice is to step back for a minute and observe the other guests. At times like these you can learn a lot by simply watching how others behave. Being classy demands that you eat slowly, little by little (if you're really hungry, it should help you to feel better knowing that little by little you'll be able to eat a lot!).

If the food is laid out on only one or two tables, don't dig a trench in front of them so you can always reach the food. Take something and back away. Think about others. Elbowing people to get to the table for an appetizer is a bit humiliating.

If you're talking with a group of people at a party and you want to move on to another group, wait for an appropriate moment. If someone speaks to you directly, try to end the conversation politely ("What you're saying about the extinction of mollusks in the Indian Sea is fascinating. Look, I was hoping to say hello to a friend I saw walk in a few minutes ago. I'm going to go talk to him for a minute, and I'll catch up with you guys later, OK?"). On the other hand, if others in the group are talking and you're just listening, it's fine to simply mutter an excuse without interrupting the conversation ("I'll be right back"). Parties are designed to get together and talk with many people, but learn how to move from one person to the other with class.

A classy person helps those putting on the party to make sure everything runs smoothly. So avoid arguments, fights, and criticism, and contribute to a positive atmosphere instead. Dance, have a good time, introduce those who don't know each other, or introduce yourself, and so on. You'll be greatly appreciated if you take charge of potentially problematic situations, such as helping someone who's had too much to drink control himself or herself or making sure the furniture doesn't get trashed. In this case James Bond still has a lot to learn (every time he goes to a party something happens).

If you happen to be the host or hostess, when it comes time for the party to end, end it subtly. Lower the music volume every few minutes and begin putting away the food and drink little by little. You can ask a few people to help you pick up. Your guests will understand that it's time to extinguish the candles—that is, to get going.

On the street

If you're carrying an umbrella because it's raining and the sidewalk is narrow, be sure to lift it up when another person walks by. That way the two umbrellas won't collide and get both of you wet. If the sidewalk is wide enough for only one person, the gentleman should step down into the road or step aside to let the lady pass by. The lady should show her thanks with a smile.

If it's raining and a guy and a girl are walking together, a guy with class should walk on the side of the sidewalk nearest the street, as the girl should do if she's with a child or older person. That way, if a car passes by and sprays water, ladies, older people, and children won't have to suffer the consequences. A guy should also walk closest to the road if the neighborhood isn't very safe—for example, if thieves might try to rob people from a car or motorcycle. In this case, guys should take responsibility (simply because they have larger physiques and can take a punch or a shove better).

At times the guy should enter a bar before the girl so he can take a quick look around to see if there's anything going on that would make her uncomfortable. It depends on the location, the neighborhood, the kind of bar it is, and whether you have been there before or not, but it's a good idea if you're in an area you aren't familiar with and it looks a little shady.

If two people arrive at the entrance to a building or room at the same time, the younger of the two should let the other go in first with a hand gesture and a smile. Guys should also hold the door open for older people and women, allowing them to enter first (except in an unfamiliar bar, as we have already mentioned). If you're entering a building, take the time to hold the door open for anyone behind you—or at least make sure it doesn't slam in someone's face.

If you're chewing gum and are tired of it, it's good manners to wrap it in a piece of paper and throw it in a wastebasket. If you stick it someplace or throw it on the floor, it will surely stick to someone else. Come to think of it, have you ever seen a cow chew grass? It's quite a spectacle, and those who chew gum with their mouths open look quite similar.

People's true colors come out when they're waiting in line. It's not easy to wait your turn. It demands self-control and respect toward others. If someone cuts in front of you, you can say something, always assuming at first that they didn't do it on purpose ("Excuse me, you may not have noticed, but the line starts over there"). If you're in a big hurry, ask those in line if it's OK to go ahead of them. If you're not in a hurry, cutting in line may seem smart to you but it's really rather smart alecky, and a smart aleck is a selfish smarty-pants.

Receiving gifts

Every time you receive a gift, say thank you, even if you already have that book, the shirt looks dreadful, the sunglasses are out of style, you have no idea what it is, or you're never going to use it. Thank the giver nonetheless. It's rude to ask how much the gift cost—you'll put the giver on the spot and make him or her feel uncomfortable. The important thing is that someone was thinking about you. Open your gift in front of the person who gave it to you. If you're lucky enough to receive many gifts, don't get overly excited about one gift in particular and forget about the rest.

Pay equal attention to each gift as you open it. Always say thank you with a smile and an appropriate sign of affection, whether it's a kiss on the cheek, a hug, an enthusiastic howl, or whatever. If the person who gave you the gift is not there (for instance, if it's from your grandma who has a kangaroo farm in Australia), send her a text message with a thousand little hearts or an email to thank her.

If people ask you what kind of gift you'd like, it's better to give them hints (for example, "I'd like a few new Playstation games"). Asking for something directly can be a little forceful. Making suggestions helps gift givers to be more confident they'll buy a gift you'll like (for example, "Today I saw some orange Nike tennis shoes that I really liked"). Saying "I don't want anything" just makes it more difficult for them.

Treat your gifts well. If you carelessly toss a sweater you were just given three minutes ago onto the couch, that shows you really don't like it. If you have to exchange a gift (because your confused aunt bought you a shirt from the football team that just lost 8-0 to your favorite team last Sunday), do it tactfully. For example, you can say, "It's a great shirt, but it's a little small, and I would love to wear it for the next game. Do you still have the receipt so I can exchange it for a bigger one? I might choose another team as well."

Those who are ill

When your friends are ill, send them a message to ask how they're feeling. Call them by phone the next day. If it's a close friend, ask him or her if it would be OK to come and visit. If the person is weak, your visit should last no longer than half an hour. Think about what you'll say while you're there. Normally when someone is sick, he or she is pretty bored, so any outside news is appreciated, and making someone laugh is even better.

If you visit sick friends at the hospital, make sure your visit doesn't wear them out. If doctors or nurses come in, tell them you'll wait outside the room until they're done (sometimes the patient may want to ask the nurse a personal question). Hospitals tend to have a quiet atmosphere, so don't come in shouting or with your music blaring. However, wearing your funeral face isn't appropriate either.

Ask the sick person briefly about his or her health, but don't go into too much detail. You also shouldn't begin talking about yourself or someone else you know who has suffered the same illness. Be positive without being naïve or dismissive ("Oh, you broke your knee? Don't worry, it's no big deal. I broke mine, too. In two days you'll be up and running, you'll see . . .").

Offer to help the parents of friends who are ill. If

your friend needs to be kept up to speed on classwork or studies, talk to your teacher. You could also bring your friend a movie, ask if you can visit again, etc.

If you're the one who is ill and someone comes to visit you (because secret agents and actresses also get sick every now and then), make sure your room is orderly and properly ventilated. Ask someone to help you if necessary. If you're visiting someone and it smells bad or the person's illness disturbs you, don't bat an eyelash. These things should be encountered stoically, without getting perturbed.

In the car

Driving fast is not driving well. Speeding is something the engine does, not you, and driving well is much easier if you don't speed. Driving well means moving along safely at a good pace, respecting traffic laws, and using common sense. Your passengers shouldn't leave the car kissing the ground and reciting a Hail Mary; you shouldn't cause other drivers to get angry, nor should you risk your life. Being a good driver is much more than merely stepping on the gas pedal.

Not everyone can drive as well as you do. Sometimes you may encounter older people who get distracted easily, parents who are attentive to small children in the backseat, and people who may be worried about many things or who aren't familiar with the area. Be patient with others who make a mistake while driving. Don't get angry with them. If their error puts other people in harm's way, let them know with class. Sometimes a smile is more effective than a string of insults and ugly gestures from your car window.

If you're the one to make a mistake behind the wheel and someone honks his horn at you, accept that you've erred, and thank the person for letting you know. Because we all have a certain level of pride, it bothers us to be corrected, but fools are the only ones who never make mistakes. It's easier to get along with those who simply admit they're wrong.

If you're driving, make sure your passengers are comfortable. Ask them whether they would like to listen to music or not, if the heat or the air is at a comfortable temperature, if they prefer the windows up or down, and so on. If someone offers you a ride somewhere, avoid repeatedly making suggestions about which road to take or commenting on the person's driving, unless your advice is specifically solicited. If you're riding in the passenger seat, it's not very classy to put your feet up on the dashboard (besides being dangerous—you'd fly out of the car like a firecracker if you were to crash). Even though you may think you look cool, I regret to inform you that you're not driving down the coast of

California in a convertible. (If you happen to be reading this book while your friends are taking you swimming on a California beach, maybe we could make an exception . . .)

Who should sit where in the car? If you're driving, the most important person or the oldest gets the front seat. The rest sit in the back. If one of your passengers lets you know he or she gets carsick, that person should ride in the front seat, and you should make sure you drive carefully.

At the beach

You should wear a swimsuit only if you're swimming or sunbathing. If you leave the beach to get something to eat or take a walk around town, put on a shirt or a cover-up. Only Tarzan and Jane have permission to walk around the jungle half-naked.

The unwritten law on the beach is that those who want to relax in peace get first dibs. Running, playing soccer, throwing a frisbee, splashing your friends, or hitting a badminton birdie around are all good activities—as long as you don't bother anyone. You should assume that most people like to spend hours lying around in the sand, doing absolutely nothing. Do your best not to get sand all over them or splash them. It's not about imposing your rights, but rather showing good manners. Loud music on the beach can give others a headache—play it only if most of the people around you are young.

If you accidentally bother people and they complain (you sprayed them with sand when you passed by, you stepped on their towel, or you were yelling too loudly), say you're sorry. You won't embarrass yourself. These situations demand that you be in control of your emotions. It's not smart to challenge the other person; pride wars always end badly. If people complain in a crude way, you can demand they show you more respect as long as you maintain your composure. For example, if a person says, "Hey! You stepped on my foot while I was sunbathing! Watch where you're going, you idiot!" you can say, "I'm really sorry; I mean it. But that doesn't give you the right to insult me. I've apologized and will be more careful, but please watch your manners."

Sometimes it looks like Attila and his barbarian friends have just been sunbathing. They leave behind plastic cups, beer bottles, Coke cans, cigarette butts, a sandal, watermelon husks, etc. You should pick up everything you brought in, and it's classy to pick up trash even if it's not yours.

At the movies

Some people go to the movies to relax. Therefore, even if you're going with a group of friends, try not to act like band of barbarians. Avoid hitting the seat in front of you, getting in and out of line repeatedly, being the jokester by talking about scenes in the movie, opening candies and chocolates really slowly, and, of course, talking throughout the movie. If you're bored out of your skull because the movie is really bad, tell your friends, "Let's give this Norwegian-Austrian psychodrama ten more minutes, and if it doesn't get any better, let's get out of here, OK?"

If someone is talking and preventing you from hearing the movie, let the person know politely by saying, "Excuse me, I can't hear the movie when you keep talking. Thank you!" Something like that is much better than being rude by saying, "Would you shut up already!". If the offender still keeps talking, let one of the theater employees know.

Avoid using your cell phone inside the theater. The light from your smartphone's screen might bother those watching the movie. If you have to take a call or check a text message, go out to the lobby.

If you've already seen the movie, don't tell those around you what's going to happen next ("Now you'll see how they kill James Bond!"). It's true that knowing what's coming up makes us feel like we have the upper hand, but for those who haven't seen it, it's pathetic (especially because everyone knows that Agent 007 never dies).

At the gym

In order to play any sport, especially a team sport, you need to have the right equipment. In addition, you shouldn't wear a watch, rings, necklaces or anything else that could hurt others while you're playing. Bring a small towel with you as well—don't use just any old rag that might be laying around.

While at the gym, don't take up all of the trainer's time and energy if he or she must also be attentive to other people. In a similar vein, it's respectful to alternate workout machines so when you finish a set you can leave it free for someone else to use. If you set the weight machine at a certain level, put it back to a neutral position when you leave.

When you walk into the locker room, it's polite to greet those present in a general fashion, without expecting a response. Don't eat in the locker rooms, and don't dillydally a long time either. It's best to talk outside. If you plan to take a shower, do so quickly and pull the shower curtain closed. Wearing flip-flops in the locker room and shower area is both good manners and good hygiene.

14

GOOD QUOTES TO USE
AS CONVERSATION STARTERS

Sow a thought, and you reap an act;
Sow an act, and you reap a habit;
Sow a habit, and you reap a character;
Sow a character, and you reap a destiny.
Samuel Smiles, Scottish writer

There is not a single serious thing that you
can't say with a smile.
Alejandro Casona, Spanish writer

Try to be punctual at all times. Those waiting for you are surely
reliving all your defects while they wait.
Nicolas Boileau, French poet

The greatness of a man is measured by how he treats
those from whom he has nothing to gain.
Ann Landers, American journalist
(originally attributed to publisher Malcolm Forbes)

It's nice to be important, but it's more important
to be nice.
José Martí, Cuban hero

Any fool can criticize, condemn or complain—and most fools do.
Dale Carnegie, American professor

Good humor may be said to be one of the very best articles
of dress one can wear in society.
William M. Thackeray, English author

Conviction is worthless unless it's converted into conduct.
Thomas Carlyle, Scottish thinker

No other folk make such a trampling [as orcs]. . . . It seems
their delight to slash and beat down growing things
that are not even in their way.
Legolas, Elf of Middle Earth, from Chapter 1
of The Two Towers by J.R.R. Tolkien

I pray you, Sir Knight, to cease a language
so commonly used by strolling minstrels that it
becomes not the mouth of knights or nobles.
Lady Rowena from Ivanhoe by Sir Walter Scott

When a man gets dressed, he covers up his body.
When a woman gets dressed, she discovers her soul.
Carlos Goñi, philosopher

A brave heart and a courteous tongue. . . . they shall carry thee
far through the jungle, manling."
Kaa, the serpent, talking with Mowgli, the jungle boy,
from The Jungle Book by Rudyard Kipling

The future has not been written. There is no fate
but what we make for ourselves.
John Connor in Terminator 3: Rise of the Machines